The Truth Seeker's Library™

This Present Earth Will One Day Be Eternal Hell!

Roger Henri Trepanier

Scripture taken from

This book is available for purchase
in print format or as an eBook
on all major distribution channels

The author may be contacted at the website:

http://www.pilgrimpathwaypublications.com

Trademarks:

Pilgrim Pathway Publications™, Servant of God Most High™, The Truth Seeker's Library™, The Practical Helps Library™, The Christian Fiction Library™, and The Word Of God Library™ are trademarks of Roger Henri Trepanier

This book is dedicated to all those on earth who by the grace, mercy, and love of God have come to believe in God through faith in His precious Son, The Lord Jesus Christ! To each of them the following is true:

"Truly, truly, I (Jesus) say to you, he who hears My word, and believes Him (God The Father) who sent Me, has eternal life, and does not come into judgment, but has passed out of death into life."

John 5:24

Titles available from Roger Henri Trepanier in The Truth Seeker's Library™ series:

God Did Not Create Human Beings To Die… But To Live On… Eternally!
Finding Comfort And Encouragement In The Promises Of God In The Last Days
How We Know For Sure That We Are Living In The Last Days!
Have You Ever Wondered What Happens After Death?
An Introduction To The New World That Is Coming On The Earth
Deeper Truths Of The Christian Life
Evangelism As God Intended
Keeping On Serving God In The Last Days
The Mysterious World Of Angels And Demons
No One Loves As He Loves!
Thanks Be To God For His Indescribable Gift!
The Church Is Very Much Alive, Well, And Growing!
Tracing The Steps Of The Son Of God From Eternity To Eternity!
War, And Going To War, Is Simply Not Of God!
God Never Meant Prayer To Be A Mystery!
Health Is One Of God's Great Blessings!
Removing The Mystery Surrounding Baptism!
This World's Return To Paganism Is Almost Complete!
Removing The Mystery Surrounding Heaven!
God's Covenants Were Meant For Mankind's Blessing!
The Four Ages Of Time
The Awesomeness Of God!
A Call To A Biblical Christianity!
Believers! Look Up! Our Homegoing Is Any Day!
Why God Created The Male And The Female!
This Earth Was Never Meant To Be The Believer's Home!
It Is A Terrifying Thing To Fall Into The Hands Of The Living God!
The Rapture Of The Church Is God's Last End Time Event!

Titles available from Roger Henri Trepanier in The Practical Helps Library™ series:

Learning to Overcome The Perplexities Of This Present Life
So, I Hear You Want To Work With Seniors?
I Will Not Have This Man To Rule Over Me!
Spiritual Truth To Warm The Heart!
Fasten Your Seatbelts: Turbulence Ahead!
Living A Normal Christian Life In An Increasingly Abnormal World!
If You Have Jesus; You Do Not Need Drugs!
To Do God's Will Is To Have A Foretaste Of Heaven!
This World Is Ready For The Rule Of The Antichrist!
President Trump And The Q Movement Versus Satan And The DEEP STATE
More Of God's Great Promises For Comfort And Encouragement!
Alert! The C-Virus Pandemic Was Satan's Practice Run For A New World Order
The Days Are Evil! The Time Is Short! Be Saved From This Perverse Generation!
Your Worldview Determines Your Wellbeing And Eternal Destiny!
What We Are Watching Is The Spirit Of The Antichrist At Work!
A Sure Cure For Loneliness!
Will God Allow President Trump To Regain The White House?
The Antichrist Arises Out Of Europe And Is About To Appear On The World Scene!

Titles available from Roger Henri Trepanier in The Christian Fiction Library™ series:

The Beginning Of A New Dawn
It Is Never Too Late For Love!
The True To Life Musings Of Fred And Ernie
Between A Rock And A Hard Place!
Love Knows No Boundaries!
A Woman Worth Pursuing!

Love Is More Than Just A Four Letter Word!
The Twists And Turns Of The Life Of Faith!

Titles available from Roger Henri Trepanier in The Word Of God Library™ series:

God's First Letter To The Thessalonians
God's Second Letter To The Thessalonians
God's Letter To Believers Through Jude
God's Three Short Letters To Believers Through John
God's Letter To Scattered Believers Through James
God's Letter To Titus
God's Prophetic Word To Mankind Through Daniel
God's Letter To Philemon And God's Letter To The Colossians
God's Consummation Of All In The Book Of Revelation
God's Letter To The Philippians
God's First Letter Through Peter
God's Second Letter Through Peter
Jonah, God's Reluctant Prophet!
God's Letter To The Galatians
God's Providence In The Book Of Esther
God's Love For Gentiles In The Book Of Ruth
God's Letter To The Ephesians
God's First Letter To Timothy
God's Second Letter To Timothy
Jesus' Sermon On The Mount: Matthews 5 to 7
Jesus" Parting Words Of Love To His Own: John 13 To 16
God's Letter To The Romans Through The Apostle Paul
God's Letter To The Hebrews

INTRODUCTION

At Acts 20 in God's word, we see the apostle Paul being led of God to say to the elders of the local church at Ephesus what we read at verses 18,20,27 in part, "[18] You yourselves know, from the first day that I set foot in Asia, how I was with you the whole time... [20] how I did not shrink from declaring to you anything that was profitable... [27] For I did not shrink from declaring to you the whole purpose of God." Therefore dear readers, this is what God's servant will be seeking to do in this book also, namely to speak of the whole counsel of God in speaking of an unpleasant subject like the fact that this present earth will one day be eternal hell!

What needs to be grasped here is that this is something that God Himself has decreed as to what will take place one day, as time ends and eternity begins again, which therefore also means that He is the only authority to consult on this truth! Since God always acts righteously and just for all of time and for eternity, we can be sure that He has good reasons for allowing or restraining evil, and eventually judging the evil doers of it, doing so in accordance with His word!

And so in this book we will look at the fact that this earth will one day become eternal hell. We will be looking at 'why' and 'how' that came to be, and also 'when' that will happen! We will be starting with God's intent for this earth at the original creation in Genesis, eventually ending in the consummation of all things in God's book of Revelation, where we will see God cast this earth from His Presence forever, after He has caused it to become eternal hell!

We are to also note that there is an Addenda at the back of the book with four sections. At Addendum A, there is a brief outline of the four ages of time, for any reading the book who might not be familiar with this information. At Addendum B, there is a brief outline of the two comings from Heaven to earth in time of God's Son, The Lord Jesus Christ, for any who may not be familiar with this information either. At Addendum C, we have an exposition of God's new creation in time; and then at Addendum D, we have a presentation of the gospel, which is the good news that God has given in His word regarding His Son, The Lord Jesus Christ, for any reader who might not as yet have this vital personal relationship with God, through faith in His Son.

What should also be mentioned before closing this Introduction, because we are all somewhat curious by nature, is that after completing 21 years of formal education and then spending almost 28 years working in Project Engineering and Management in the Corporate offices of two large utilities, God called His servant as a non-denominational evangelist in early 1999, and then sent him out over two thousand miles, away from family and friends, to the place of service God assigned, which is where His servant has been, and is still serving Him, as evangelist, author, and counselor. The author is a widower with three adopted children, all now married with a family of their own.

Please note the two websites listed below, which have been established for the purpose of interacting with readers and for gospel ministry:

http://www.pilgrimpathwaypublications.com

http://servantofmosthigh.com

And now my prayer is that God will richly bless you as you read this book, and greatly minister to every need in your life, as only God can! To Him be all praise, honor, and glory, with thanksgiving, both now and forevermore! Amen.

CONTENTS

“In the beginning God created the heavens and the earth.”

Genesis 1:1

“Then God said, "Let Us make man in Our image, according to Our likeness; and let them rule over the fish of the sea and over the birds of the sky and over the cattle and over all the earth, and over every creeping thing that creeps on the earth."”

Genesis 1:26

“God saw all that He had made, and behold, it was very good. And there was evening and there was morning, the sixth day.”

Genesis 1:31

CHAPTER ONE

What God's design was for this earth at the time of the original creation!

As we begin this most revealing book, we need to start when God first brought this original creation into existence and see what God's design was for this present earth at that time! And so, at Genesis 1:1 we have God declare, "In the beginning God created the heavens and the earth," where we see God bring this present earth into existence, including its two created heavens, the one that is seen and which relates to this earth; while the other is unseen and was created to be the home of the angelic beings.

We then see in the rest of Genesis 1 that all that presently exists was brought into existence by God in six literal days of creation, with God being then able to say after those six literal days, as we read at Genesis 1:31, "God saw all that He had made, and behold, it was very good. And there was evening and there was morning, the sixth day." The important truth to remember here is that "it was very good" in God's sight simply because there was NO SIN PRESENT anywhere in all God's creation; not in humanity, nor in any of the angelic beings that had also now come into existence!

There is something else that we need to be aware of here from Genesis 1, which directly relates to our present subject, and it is to note what God said at Genesis 1:26, where we read, "Then God said, "Let Us (that is, Father, Son, and Holy

Spirit) make man in Our image, according to Our likeness; and LET THEM RULE OVER the fish of the sea and over the birds of the sky and over the cattle and over all the earth, and over every creeping thing that creeps on the earth."" What we see occurring here, which is very important to keep in mind, is that we see God giving mankind THE RULE over this present earth, which meant over all that had been brought into existence by God during those six days of creation, and which would now be part of this earth!

The TWO KEY TRUTHS to keep in mind from this present chapter then is that there was NO SIN, which also meant no evil, anywhere in Gods creation; and also that GOD HAD GIVEN MANKIND THE RULE OVER THIS PRESENT EARTH!

"The Lord God commanded the man, saying, "From any tree of the garden you may eat freely; but from the tree of the knowledge of good and evil you shall not eat, for in the day that you eat from it you will surely die.""

Genesis 2:16,17

"When the woman saw that the tree was good for food, and that it was a delight to the eyes, and that the tree was desirable to make one wise, she took from its fruit and ate; and she gave also to her husband with her, and he ate."

Genesis 3:6

CHAPTER TWO

The saddest day of all world history!

And now that we know the two key truths we learned from Genesis 1, we can go on to Genesis 2, where we see that God now gives greater detail to some of the events which took place during those six days of creation at Genesis 1, with God now especially focusing on MANKIND, because this is the pinnacle of God's creation, for as we have seen at Genesis 1:26 earlier, only mankind was made in the image and likeness of God when first created!

And so, after God tells us how the first man, Adam, was created at Genesis 2:7, being of three constituent parts, namely a body, a spirit, and a soul (also noting 1 Thessalonians 5:23). From this we are to know that the spirit was for mankind to be able to commune with God, Who is a spirit Being (noting John 4:24); while the soul was for the purpose of being able to commune with other human beings; while the physical body is simply the temporary part of human beings that God designed to hold the immortal spirit and soul, and will only last for as long as one is on this present earth!

And since the first man, Adam, was as yet an INNOCENT human being, in terms of not knowing good or evil, God prepared the GARDEN OF EDEN here on earth as a place of TESTING for the first man. So after placing Adam in that garden of Eden, as we see at Genesis 2:8, God then makes it known at Genesis 2:9 that He had two special trees in the garden of Eden, as we now there read, “Out of the ground the Lord God caused to grow EVERY TREE that is pleasing to the sight and GOOD FOR FOOD; THE TREE OF LIFE also in the midst of the garden, and THE TREE OF THE KNOWLEDGE OF GOOD AND EVIL.”

What we see from this verse of God’s word then is that there were THREE KINDS OF TREES in the garden of Eden, where God was now in the process of testing the first man, Adam. The first mentioned was the tree that was good for food in order to maintain the physical body. The next tree mentioned is the tree of life. Since God is an eternal Being, in that He has always existed, and therefore has no beginning or end, then we are to see that in partaking of the tree of life Adam would have and maintain eternal life with God!

We then see that the third tree mentioned is the tree of the knowledge of good and evil, which we are now to see from Genesis 2:16,17 that God forbade Adam from partaking of, which was now God’s test of Adam – who was here representative of the whole human race, in that any other human being would have done the same thing as we eventually see Adam do – as we now there read, “[16] THE LORD GOD COMMANDED THE MAN, saying, "From any tree of the garden you may eat freely; [17] BUT FROM THE TREE OF THE KNOWLEDGE OF GOOD AND EVIL YOU SHALL NOT EAT, for in the day that you eat from it you will surely die."” And so, God’s test of Adam was whether he would OBEY GOD’S COMMAND!

What God did next, as we see from Genesis 2:18-25, is to make Eve out of one of Adam’s ribs, for God had said at Genesis 2:18, “It is not good for the man to be alone; I will make him A HELPER suitable for him."” And so, as we come to Genesis 3, we have both Adam and Eve in the garden of Eden, still both innocent, in that neither one of them had sinned by partaking of the tree of the knowledge of good and evil.

However, what is also key for us to know here is that there was something else that occurred in God’s original creation, AFTER God had said that all was very good at Genesis 1:31, which is that SIN DID OCCUR IN THE SPIRITUAL REALM of the second created heaven, where the angelic beings were! For what we now need to note is that when the devil was created by God, he was a sinless angelic being who had access to the very Presence of God, along with all the other angelic beings. However, there came a day when PRIDE did take over in him and he sinned against God, then becoming Satan, the devil, who then led a third of the other angelic beings in rebellion against God (noting Revelation 12:4).

So let us note to begin with what God tells us about the fall of this angelic being into sin, who after he sinned became, Satan, the devil, noting now what God tells us of him at Isaiah 14:12-14, especially noting his five "I will" here, "[12] How you have fallen from heaven, O star of the morning, son of the dawn! You have been cut down to the earth, you who have weakened the nations! [13] But you said in your heart, 'I WILL ascend to heaven; I WILL raise my throne above the stars of God, And I WILL sit on the mount of assembly in the recesses of the north. [14] I WILL ascend above the heights of the clouds; I WILL make myself like the Most High."

Then let us note what God goes on to further tell us at Ezekiel 28:12-17 in part, regarding that angelic being who became Satan, the devil, there reading, "[12] You had the seal of perfection, full of wisdom and perfect in beauty. [13] You were in Eden, the garden of God; every precious stone was your covering... On the day that you were CREATED they were prepared. [14] You were the anointed cherub (an order of angelic beings with a higher rank than ordinary angels) who covers, and I placed you there. You were on the holy mountain of God; you walked in the midst of the stones of fire. [15] YOU WERE BLAMELESS IN YOUR WAYS FROM THE DAY YOU WERE CREATED UNTIL UNRIGHTEOUESNESS (the sin of pride) WAS FOUND IN YOU. [16] By the abundance of your trade you were internally filled with violence, and YOU SINNED, therefore I have cast you as profane from the mountain of God. And I have destroyed you, O covering cherub, from the midst of the stones of fire. [17] YOUR HEART WAS LIFTED UP

BECAUSE OF YOUR BEAUTY, YOU CORRUPTED YOUR WISDOM BY REASON OF YOUR SPLENDOR..."

From the verses in Isaiah and also from Ezekiel here, we see that from the time of his own fall into sin, which was due to pride, SATAN, THE DEVIL, HAS HAD THE AMBITION OF NOT ONLY BEING LIKE GOD, IN TERMS OF ALSO HAVING A KINGDOM ON EARTH, but of actually having his throne higher than God's throne, SO AS TO RULE NOT ONLY OVER GOD, BUT ALSO TO RULE OVER ALL OF GOD'S ORIGINAL CREATION!

In now knowing these truths, we can now turn to Genesis 3:1-6 and see what now happened here on earth in the most infamous day in all world history, noting now what we there read, "[1] Now THE SERPENT was more crafty than any beast of the field which the Lord God had made. AND HE SAID TO THE WOMAN, "Indeed, has God said, 'You shall not eat from any tree of the garden'?" [2] THE WOMAN SAID TO THE SERPENT, "From the fruit of the trees of the garden we may eat; [3] but from the fruit of the tree which is in the middle of the garden, God has said, 'You shall not eat from it or touch it, or you will die.' " [4] The serpent said to the woman, "You surely will not die! [5] For God knows that in the day you eat from it your eyes will be opened, and you will be like God, KNOWING GOOD AND EVIL." [6] When the woman saw that the tree was good for food, and that it was a delight to the eyes, and that the tree was desirable to make one wise, SHE TOOK FROM ITS FRUIT AND ATE; AND SHE GAVE ALSO TO HER HUSBAND WITH HER, AND HE ATE."

There are three very important truths that we are to observe from this passage, relating specifically to our present subject. The first truth to notice is that "the serpent" in this passage here is none else but Satan, the devil, who had by this point in time already committed the first sin to occur in God's original sinless creation! We know this here based on what God later tells us at Revelation 12:9, where we read, "And the great dragon was thrown down, the serpent of old who is called the devil and Satan, who deceives the whole world; he was thrown down to the earth, and his angels were thrown down with him."

Then the second very important truth to notice is that Satan came to Eve, and not to Adam, in order to tempt her into sinning against God by partaking of the forbidden tree. We know this based on what God also later tells us at 2 Corinthians 11:3 in part, "But I am afraid that, as the serpent deceived Eve by his craftiness...," and then also at 1 Timothy 2:14, where we read, "And it was not Adam who was deceived, but the woman being deceived, fell into transgression." And so, we see that Eve's sin was exactly the same as that of the devil, by which we have seen he also sinned against God, which was the sin of pride! God made Eve to be Adam's helper, not the chief spokesman and head of their family! Adam's sin, when he partook of the forbidden tree was DISOBEDIENCE TO GOD'S DIRECT COMMAND TO HIM, as we have seen at Genesis 2:16,17!

And then the third and most important truth to notice here for our present purpose is that we have already seen from Genesis 1:26 that GOD HAD GIVEN MANKIND THE RULE OVER THIS PRESENT EARTH! But we have also seen that the devil's ambition was not only to be like God and to seek to be over Him, but also to rule over this earth and all of God's creation, including mankind! What this means then is that when Adam and Eve sinned, who had the rule over this present earth and all it contains, THEY SIDED WITH THE DEVIL, WHICH MEANT THAT THEY EFFECTIVELY TURNED THE RULE OVER THIS EARTH AND ALL IT CONTAINS OVER TO SATAN, THE DEVIL!

We know this because of what God records Satan, the devil, as saying to His Son later, once He had come from Heaven to earth and taken on our humanity, noting now what we read at Luke 4:5-7, "[5] And he led Him up and SHOWED HIM ALL THE KINGDOMS OF THE WORLD in a moment of time. [6] And the devil said to Him, "I will give You all this domain and its glory; FOR IT HAS BEEN HANDED OVER TO ME, AND I GIVE IT TO WHOMEVER I WISH. [7] Therefore if You worship before me, it shall all be Yours."

And so, the very important truth to remember from this present chapter is that when Adam and Eve sinned against God in the garden of Eden here on earth, they effectively turned over the rule over this present earth over to Satan, the devil, who still has that rule to the present day!

"Out of the ground the Lord God caused to grow every tree that is pleasing to the sight and good for food; the tree of life also in the midst of the garden, and the tree of the knowledge of good and evil."

Genesis 2:9

CHAPTER THREE

What the significance was relating to mankind partaking of the tree of the knowledge of good and evil!

In this chapter, we will be looking at the significance of the partaking of the tree of the knowledge of good and evil in relation to mankind and the angelic being known as Satan, the devil. We need to recall that in the previous chapter we saw that God had told Adam NOT to eat of the tree of the knowledge of good and evil at Genesis 2:16,17.

However, when the devil, in the form of a serpent, came to Adam and Eve in the garden of Eden, he told them to go ahead and eat from the tree of the knowledge of good and evil, noting from Genesis 3:5 the reason he gives them for doing so, "For God knows that in the day you eat from it your eyes will be opened, and you will be like God, knowing good and evil." The devil here promises Adam and Eve to "be like God" if they eat of the forbidden tree. Unfortunately, the reverse was to be the truth, for Adam and Eve would now be like the devil in sinning against God, for their sin against God meant rebellion against Him, just as the devil's committal of that original sin meant he was in rebellion against God!

God's precious Son, The Lord Jesus Christ, pointed this truth out one day when He was here on earth at His first coming, noting what He said to the unbelievers of His day at John 8:44, "You are of your father the devil, and you want to do the desires of your father. He was a murderer from the beginning (in having filled Cain with hatred for Abel, so as to murder him), and does not stand in the truth because there is no truth in him. Whenever he speaks a lie, he speaks from his own nature, for he is a liar and the father of lies." All those who sin are therefore to be seen as making themselves children of the devil, noting what God further tells us at 1 John 3:8 in part, "the one who practices sin is of the devil; for the devil has sinned from the beginning."

And so we are to see that while God was out to make mankind into His own image and likeness, the devil was out to pervert that by seeking to have mankind be after his own image and likeness through sin! God does tell us at Revelation 12:9 that the devil "deceives the whole world," for he is a deceiver, and one of his primary tools by which he works is deception! We are to see that it is only from God that mankind can learn what is "good," for only God is good (noting Psalm 34:8 and Psalm 100:5); and that is only from the devil that mankind can learn what is "evil," for that is what the devil is the father of!

"For what does it profit a man to gain the whole world, and forfeit his soul?"

Mark 8:36

"Then the Lord saw that the wickedness of man was great on the earth, and that every intent of the thoughts of his heart was only evil continually. The Lord was sorry that He had made man on the earth, and He was grieved in His heart."

Genesis 6:5,6

CHAPTER FOUR

Why there is a hell, and why it will be this present earth!

In this chapter we will look at WHY there is a hell, and also WHY it is to be this present earth! As to the answer for why God chose to have this present earth be eternal hell is that THIS IS WHERE SIN OCCURRED and has been occurring since Adam and Eve sinned that first sin to occur here on earth! This earth is also where unbelievers of time have resided and will reside to the end of the ages of time! This means that this earth is not only polluted through and through with evil, but this is also where innocent blood has been shed, from the blood of innocent children, to God's own innocent and sinless Son, The Lord Jesus Christ!

Then as to the primary reason that can be given for WHY THERE IS A HELL is that the entry of sin into God's perfect and sinless creation meant that some of mankind would die physically after a certain period of time on earth, for the penalty for sin is death, as God had said to Adam at Genesis 2:17; which is a truth repeated again by God at Roman 6:23, reading there in part, "For the wages of sin is death…" What this means then is that some human beings will die physically without ever coming to believe in God's precious Son, The Lord Jesus Christ, which is THE ONLY WAY OF ESCAPE FROM HELL! In other words, there has to be a hell for all the unbelievers of time, which of course includes Satan, the devil, and all the fallen angels with him!

Let us note what God's Son said to the unbelievers of His day, as recorded for us at John 8:21,24, where we read, "[21] Then He said again to them, "I go away, and you will seek Me, and WILL DIE IN YOUR SINS, WHERE I AM GOING, YOU CANNOT COME... [24] Therefore I said to you that you will die in your sins; FOR UNLESS YOU BELIEVE THAT I AM HE, YOU WILL DIE IN YOUR SINS."

What is very important to grasp here is that WHERE God's Son was going – after His death at the cross as payment due the sins of the human race, His burial, and then His resurrection from the dead the third day, followed by His subsequent ascension – was back to Heaven again, which is God's eternal and uncreated dwelling place. And we also notice here that He knew that NOT ALL human beings born into this present physical world will come to personally know God in salvation, through faith in Him while on earth and before physical death came (noting 2 Thessalonians 3:3; 2:10). And since these unbelievers would die in their sins without ever personally knowing God in salvation meant that they could not go to Heaven, since Heaven is God's home, and since these unbelievers were in the rebellion due to sin all their lives while here on earth!

What needs to be grasped by all here is that when an unbeliever rejects God's Son, The Lord Jesus Christ, in this world, then one is of one's own free will rejecting Heaven and freely choosing to go to hell. I personally experienced this one day in my ministry, for there was once a man that I was witnessing to and his response to my witness was: "My friends are all going to be in hell, and that is where I want to go also!" What is revealing is that I had been speaking to him about faith in The Lord Jesus Christ, and had not even mentioned hell at all, yet he consciously was aware that the penalty for rejecting God's Son was hell!.

Another reason why there is a hell, and why it will be this present earth, is due to the fact that the sin that has been committed on this earth since the time of Adam and Eve has been ENORMOUS, and not just enormous, but TRULY DEPRAVED AND EVIL! For instance, there are videos going around of adults and children being murdered for their organs, which are then sold. And also think of the millions of children worldwide who have died through abortions! Then there is also human sex trafficking and pedophilia on a scale unimaginable! What is most appalling and repulsing here is that these sins are being committed against the most innocent, vulnerable, and defenseless among us! And of course, these sins did not start in our day, but things such as child sacrifices have been going on since the time of Adam and Eve!

Let us notice what God says about the state of the world at Genesis 6:5, "Then the Lord saw that the wickedness of man was great on the earth, and that every intent of the thoughts of his heart was only evil continually." And let us not forget that when God's own sinless Son was on earth at His first coming from Heaven, He was crucified on a cross, being rejected by the majority of those on earth at that time; for we need to remember that the nation of Israel, which rejected Him, was only a representative nation of all the nations of the earth, so that God knew that what that one nation did, any other nation would have done likewise had it been in its place! We have the proof of that today in the fact that the great majority of the people of the nations of the earth would likewise reject and crucify God's Son over again were He alive on earth today!

Another reason for why there needs to be a hell is that God is not only Creator and Provider of all that is good, but God is also Judge of all that is evil. What this means then is that if there were no punishment for all the sin and evil of earth in time, then God would not be just, in that He would be treating unbelievers in the same way as He treats believers. In order to have justice, there must be the application of God's judgment on those who sin against God and His law, which He has made known in His word, the Bible! If God did not judge righteously as He always does, then He would be seen to be as lawless as Satan, the devil, and the unbelievers of this world, who are all under the evil one's control!

We need to ever remember that God is Holy, which means without sin, and also Impeccable, that is, unable to even sin, so that what is sinful, and therefore evil in His sight, cannot even be in His Presence! Let us note what God says for instance at Jeremiah 17:4,5 in part, “[4]...For you have kindled a fire in My anger, which will burn forever. [5] Thus says the Lord, "Cursed is the man who trusts in mankind and makes flesh his strength, and whose heart turns away from the Lord.” And so, that is why believers are told at Hebrews 12:29, “for our God is a consuming fire.”

And this leads us to the fact that there have always been unbelievers on this earth from the time of Adam and Eve onward, starting with their first offspring, Cain, which means that there will always be human beings on this earth who are willing to side with the devil against God! What this means is that not all human beings born into this world in time will be saved, which further means that if God were to continue this present earth forever, then this condition just described would never change.

And so, God in His wisdom and foreknowledge established four ages to time, to allow sin to run its course and mankind to be tested through these four ages, with God making more and more of Himself known through those ages, by means of not only His word written (the Bible), but also His Word made flesh (His Son), so that at the end of recorded time, God might judge mankind, which at that point would not have any excuse before God for one’s sin and rebellion against Him! And so, God will then be seen as ever Holy and Righteous in His judgment as He casts from His Presence forever this present earth, which would by then have become eternal hell, having on it all unbelievers of time and also all fallen angelic beings!

“If your right eye makes you stumble, tear it out and throw it from you; for it is better for you to lose one of the parts of your body, than for your whole body to be thrown into hell.”

Matthew 5:29

“If your eye causes you to stumble, throw it out; it is better for you to enter the kingdom of God with one eye, than, having two eyes, to be cast into hell, where their worm does not die, and the fire is not quenched.”

Mark 9:47,48

"But I will warn you whom to fear: fear the One who, after He has killed, has authority to cast into hell; yes, I tell you, fear Him!"

Luke 12:5

CHAPTER FIVE

Grasping the reality of what hell is!

Based on what we have seen in the previous chapter, it should be obvious to all that hell is to be A PLACE OF PUNISHMENT OF THE UNBELIEVERS OF TIME! Let us note what God says at Proverbs 10:16, "The wages of the righteous (that is, believers) is life, the income of the wicked (that is, unbelievers), punishment."

And what is important to grasp about that punishment that awaits unbelievers in hell is that it will be ETERNAL! What that means is that when one is in hell, ONE NEVER COMES OUT! Let us note what God says about hell at Jude 1:7, "just as Sodom and Gomorrah and the cities around them, since they in the same way as these indulged in gross immorality and went after strange flesh, are exhibited as an example in undergoing the PUNISHMENT OF ETERNAL fire."

If one wants to know HOW LONG ETERNITY IS, then one only needs to stand by the shore of any ocean on earth and hold a drop of water in one's hand as one looks at that ocean, for that drop of water represents one's lifetime on earth and just think how many drops of water there are in that ocean!

Then we are also to grasp that hell is not only a place of punishment, but also A PLACE OF TORMENT. And since hell is forever, then this means that this torment will also be FOREVER! Let us notice that at Jude 1:7 quoted above, God there said that one's punishment, speaking of being in hell, would be by "ETERNAL FIRE." As everyone knows fire burns and is one of the worst pains that one can experience. Yet that is what hell will consist of, namely fire!

Let us note what God's Son warned unbelievers of His day about at Matthew 18:8, "If your hand or your foot causes you to stumble, cut it off and throw it from you; it is better for you to enter life crippled or lame, than to have two hands or two feet and be cast into THE ETERNAL FIRE." In other words, human beings should do all they can while on earth and still alive to avoid hell at all costs, with the only way of escape from hell being salvation through faith in God's Son, The Lord Jesus Christ, thereby obtaining the forgiveness of sins and eternal life with God forever after this life!

It is important to grasp that all unbelievers of the ages of time will die physically and then will face God at the last judgment of time, as we see at Revelation 20:11-15. Let us note what God says at Hebrews 9:27 in this regard, "And inasmuch as it is appointed for men (all unbelievers of time) to die once (speaking of physical death) and after this comes (God's) judgment..."

This is being mentioned here because when God does cast all unbelievers of time into that fire of hell here on earth after that last judgment, EVERY UNBELIEVER WILL BE THERE BODILY, THAT IS WITH A BODY THAT HAS BEEN RESURRECTED AND IS NO LONGER SUBJECT TO PHYSICAL DEATH! What that means then is that the torment that all unbelievers will experience in hell will be BODILY, and will be forever and ever!

Let us note what God's Son also told unbelievers of His day at Matthew 10:28, "Do not fear those who kill the body but are unable to kill the soul; but rather fear Him (God The Father) who is able to destroy both soul AND BODY IN HELL." And please keep in mind that the word "destroy" here does not mean annihilation, that is, putting out of existence, but rather refers to one's wellbeing being taken away, which in this case is forever!

The reality facing all human beings ever born into this world is that one will either believe in God's precious Son, The Lord Jesus Christ, before leaving this earth in physical death, and so will enter God's Presence in Heaven the moment physical death comes; or else one will consciously reject God's Son while on earth, and then one will find oneself on the way to eternal hell the moment one dies physically. Since one refused to believe and so serve God's Son willingly while on earth; now one who is an unbeliever at physical death will serve the devil eternally in hell!

""Then He will also say to those on His left, 'Depart from Me, accursed ones, into the eternal fire which has been prepared for the devil and his angels...'"

Matthew 25:41

"...For you have kindled a fire in My anger, which will burn forever."

Jeremiah 17:4 in part

CHAPTER SIX

Grasping the fact that God already has the fire of hell burning below the surface of this present earth, which will eventually cover the whole of this earth!

We have already stated that the first sin to enter God's perfect, and therefore sinless original creation, was through an angelic being who then became Satan, the devil. What we are to grasp for our present purpose is that the moment that this angelic being sinned that sin, God established THE FIRE OF HELL, FAR BELOW THE SURFACE OF THIS PRESENT EARTH that we are now living on!

To see this, let us note two verses that God gives us in His word, one being in the New Testament and the other in the Old Testament. So let us note what God tells us at Matthew 25:41 to begin with, where we read, "Then He (God's Son) will also say to those on His left (unbelievers of time at the time of the judgment of nations at the second stage of His second coming), 'Depart from Me, accursed ones, into THE ETERNAL FIRE WHICH HAS BEEN PREPARED FOR THE DEVIL AND HIS ANGELS." So when the devil sinned that first sin against God, being also when other angels went astray from God, God established a fire that will burn for all eternity, with that fire being far below the surface of this present earth!

And now let us also note what God tells us at Deuteronomy 32:22 in the Old Testament, where we read, "FOR A FIRE IS KINDLED IN MY ANGER, AND BURNS TO THE LOWEST PART OF SHEOL, AND CONSUMES THE EARTH WITH ITS YIELD, and sets on fire the foundations of the mountains." The fire that is said here to be kindled in God's anger due to sin having occurred in His sinless creation, is the same fire which God has in view at Matthew 25:41, which was kindled when the devil sinned the first sin in God's original sinless creation! And so we are to see here that this fire is now burning in the lowest part of Sheol/Hades deep below the surface of the present earth, and will one day cover the whole earth.

What is important to note here is that the word "Sheol" mentioned above is the Old Testament word for its New Testament equivalent rendered as "Hades." In other words, Sheol and Hades are speaking of the same place in God's word, which is to be seen as being deep below the surface of the present earth, where the fire of hell is already burning and will continue to burn until the end of time!

Another truth which is important to know here is that the reason that Sheol/Hades is under the present earth is because it relates to human beings who SINNED ON EARTH during the ages of time. In other words, since the first sin of mankind took place on earth, then God prepared Sheol/Hades as a place to deal with the sin of mankind DURING THE AGES OF TIME, before the final judgment of God takes place at the end of time, as we will see in the next chapter! That such a place as Sheol/Hades exists below the surface of this present earth is clear from what God says at Philippians 2:10 relating to this, "so that at the name of Jesus every knee will bow, OF THOSE WHO ARE in heaven and on earth AND UNDER THE EARTH..."

Another important truth to know about Sheol/Hades is that this place has to do with the afterlife, and so has to do with THE SPIRIT AND SOUL OF HUMAN BEINGS, AND NEVER WITH THE PHYSICAL BODY! Therefore it is important to remember that the spirit and the soul are invisible and immaterial, which makes it easy for God to move a spirit and a soul of a physically dead body to Sheol/Hades under the earth without having to dig a hole to get there!

Then another important truth to keep in mind is that Sheol/Hades has THREE COMPARTMENTS in it, one for the soul of believers, a second for the spirit and soul of unbelievers, and a third for the devil and the other fallen angels with him. And it is important to realize that these three compartments are on top of each other, with the compartment for the soul of believers being at the top, while the compartment for the devil and his fallen angels is at the bottom, where the fire of the eventual hell is already burning. There is also an IMPASSAPLE CHASM between the compartment of the believers and that of the unbelievers.

That there are such compartments in Sheol/Hades, and that it is below the surface of the present earth, can be gathered from what God says in His word, the Bible, learning for instance what A BELIEVER is recorded as saying to God at Psalm 16:10, "For You will not abandon MY SOUL IN SHEOL; nor will You allow Your Holy One to undergo decay," then also at Psalm 49:15, "But God will redeem MY SOUL FROM THE POWER OF SHEOL, for He will receive me."

The reason that the soul of a believer goes to Sheol/Hades after physical death is that it is in the soul that one's sinful nature inherited from Adam resides, which is activated when one sins that first sin against God at the age of accountability. And since that sinful nature is not removed from the believer's soul by God until the time of one's part in the first resurrection relating to believers, then if one dies before that first resurrection, then one's body goes to the grave here on earth, while the spirit goes to God, and the soul goes to Sheol/Hades. Then at the time of that first resurrection, a believer is raised from the dead with a new spiritual body to enter God's Presence in Heaven, and it is at that time that the sinful nature of the believer is removed by God! If there are any readers who would like to read more regarding what happens at the time of death and afterwards, please see the author's book, "Have you ever wondered what happens after death."

Then in regard to the fact that the spirit and soul of UNBELEVERS will also be Sheol/Hades, but in a different compartment, we are to note what God says to us at Job 21:13,14, "[13] They spend their days in prosperity, and suddenly THEY GO DOWN TO SHEOL. [14] They say to God, 'Depart from us! We do not even desire the knowledge of Your ways," and we can also see this from the example that God's Son gives at Luke 16:19-31, regarding what happens to Lazarus and the rich man after death!

And so, THE FIRE OF HELL IS ALREADY BURNING in Sheol and Hades, which is deep below the surface of this present earth, where it will continue to burn until the end of time, when, after the final judgment of Revelation 20:11-15, THAT FIRE WILL THEN RISE LIKE LAVA IN A VOLCANO AND COVER THE SURFACE OF THE WHOLE EARTH, including both created heavens, wherever sin left a footprint during time, as is clear from the last part of Deuteronomy 32:22 quoted above in the words, "and consumes the earth with its yield, and sets on fire the foundations of the mountains."

What has just been stated is a truth that God makes clear at 2 Peter 3:7, where we read, "But by His word THE PRESENT HEAVENS AND EARTH ARE BEING RESERVED FOR FIRE, KEPT FOR THE DAY OF JUDGMENT AND DESTRUCTION OF UNGODLY MEN." The fire of hell from below this earth will not cover this present earth until the final judgment of God at Revelation 20:11-15 has taken place, which is when God raises all the unbelievers of the four ages of time from the dead – since all unbelievers of time will have died physically, noting Hebrews 9:27 – and now gives them bodies to last forever, and then casts them into the lake of fire, which is hell, at which time the fire from below the earth will have engulfed this present earth. SO ETERNAL HELL IS THEN SEEN TO BE THIS PRESENT EARTH! But simultaneous to this present earth being turned into eternal hell for all unbelievers of time, and also all the fallen angelic beings, God will have created the new heavens and new earth for His new creation, which are all the believers of time!

So let us be clear that this earth was earmarked by God as being hell forever when sin first occurred at the beginning of creation, and was therefore never intended by God as the believer's home! And let us also be clear that hell is a literal place of torment, which God reserved only for all the unbelievers of time and also for all the fallen angelic beings, and that unbelieves will be there BODILY, noting now what we read at Matthew 5:30, "If your right hand makes you stumble, cut it off and throw it from you; for it is better for you to lose one of the parts of your body, THAN FOR YOUR WHOLE BODY TO GO INTO HELL." So let us note here that God emphasizes the fact that it is bodily that one goes to hell!

Another passage which would be instructive for us to note is what God says at Hebrews 10:26,27, where we read, "[26] For if we go on sinning willfully after receiving the knowledge of the truth, there no longer remains a sacrifice for sins, [27] but a terrifying expectation of judgment and the FURY OF A FIRE WHICH WILL CONSUMME THE ADVERSARIES," and then also further noting what God says in this regard at 2 Thessalonians 1:8,9, "[8] dealing out retribution to THOSE WHO DO NOT KNOW GOD and to those who do not obey the gospel of our Lord Jesus. [9] THESE WILL PAY THE PENALTY OF ETERNAL DESTRUCTION, AWAY FROM THE PRESENSE OF THE LORD, and from the glory of His power..." The word "destruction" here refers to eternal loss of wellbeing, not of being, as unbelievers do go on forever in hell, due to the fact that they have an eternal soul and spirit which cannot die, and are then given a body by God at the final judgment that will never die either!

"And inasmuch as it is appointed for men to die once and after this comes judgment..."

Hebrews 9:27

CHAPTER SEVEN

Looking in detail at the last judgment of God at the end of time, where we see God turn this earth and its heavens into eternal hell, before then casting them from His Presence forever!

What we now want to do in this chapter is to look at God's last judgment of time in detail in order to see what happens to unbelievers of time, which is to see them being cast by God into the lake of fire, which is hell, and then where we see this earth and its two created heavens being cast away from His Presence forever!

And so, after having just disposed of the devil forever in the lake of fire in the abyss deep below the surface of this present earth (noting Revelation 20:10), God now has His final judgment of time at Revelation 20:11-15, which relates ONLY TO ALL THE UNBELIEVERS OF THE FOUR AGES OF TIME, there reading, "[11] Then I saw a great white throne and Him who sat upon it, from whose presence earth and heaven fled away, and no place was found for them. [12] And I saw the dead, the great and the small, standing before the throne, and books were opened; and another book was opened, which is the book of life; and the dead were judged from the things which were written in the books, according to their deeds. [13] And the sea gave up the dead which were in it, and death and Hades gave up the dead which were in them; and they were judged, every one of them according to their deeds." [14] Then death and Hades were thrown into the lake of fire. This is the second death, the lake of fire. [15] And if anyone's name was not found written in the book of life, he was thrown into the lake of fire."

What we need to grasp here first of all is that that the apostle John, who was chosen to write down for us this word from God, sees "a great white throne," which we must realize is a throne that God establishes OUTSIDE OF HEAVEN, as His uncreated and eternal abode, which is here for the purpose of judging all the unbelievers of time all at once in this final judgment at the end of time.

It is very important that we grasp here that this white throne CANNOT be in Heaven, simply because no unbelievers can ever enter there. This cannot be Heaven since this is the final judgment of time dealing with all the unbelievers of time, who are all still in their sin, which makes it an impossibility for them to enter there! This also cannot be the first created heaven associated with the earth, for we see at verse 20:11 that it flees away from God's Presence with the earth. So this leaves only the second created heaven, as where this final judgment of God takes place!

And then John goes on and says at verse 20:11 that he saw "Him who sat upon it," and we are to realize that the "Him" here is speaking of God The Father, Who is always invisible, always indwelling His Son, Who is, here and always the visible expression of God (noting Colossians 1:15; Hebrews 1:3). That this is so can be gathered from what God tells us about this final judgment at Acts 17:31, "... He (God The Father) has fixed a day in which He (God The Father) will judge the world in righteousness through a Man (God's Son, The Lord Jesus Christ) whom He has appointed, having furnished proof to all men by raising Him from the dead."

And this throne is called a "white throne," to indicate the sinlessness of The Person sitting on the throne, Who is God's Son, for the word "white" being "Leukos," indicates that holiness here. For instance, at Matthew 17:2 God's Son is seen in glory as having white garments; as is the case also with unfallen angels, when appearing on earth at John 20:12;

and also what all believers will have in glory, once in their new resurrected bodies, as we see at Revelation 3:3,4, once the sinful nature has been removed from the soul. They too will then be sinless like God!

What is also important to grasp here from verse 20:11 is that when God says, "from whose presence earth and heaven fled away, and no place was found for them," He is indicating what happens to this present earth and its heaven once this final judgment is completed, which is after Revelation 20:15. In other words, this is so for the simple reason that all the elements mentioned from verses 20:12 to 15 are all associated with sin and the devil, with all the unrepentant and unbelieving of the human race, and so will be cast from God's Presence forever after this final judgment, which includes this present earth and everything associated with the first created heaven, such as the sun, moon, and stars!

And what is critical to remember regarding Revelation 20:12,13 is that we now have God's final judgment in time relating to ALL the unbelievers of every age all at the same time. Since, as we have noted from Hebrews 9:27, ALL unbelievers do die physically before this point in time, as the first part of God's judgment of them for rejecting Him through rejecting His Son – Whom He did put forth as The Savior of mankind in His death for our sins, His burial, and His resurrection from the dead on behalf of a sinful human race – then what is in view here is a resurrection from the dead in order to stand before God to answer for their sins, especially that of UNBELIEF. Since all unbelievers of the four ages of time refused to believe in God's Son during their stay on earth – Who suffered God's wrath due mankind's sins at the cross when He died in mankind's place – then now they will be standing before God to answer for their own sin and bear the penalty due their sins!

That there is a resurrection from the dead of unbelievers, which does take place here, is to be seen from what God tells us in His word, starting at Daniel 12:2, where we read, "Many of those who sleep in the dust of the ground will awake, these to everlasting life, but the others to disgrace and everlasting contempt," then also at John 5:28,29, where we read, "[28] Do not marvel at this; for an hour is coming, in which all who are in the tombs will hear His voice, [29] and will come forth; those who did the good deeds to a resurrection of life, those who committed the evil deeds to a resurrection of judgment," and then also at Acts 24:15, adding verse 14 for context, "[14] But this I admit to you, that according to the Way which they call a sect I do serve the God of our fathers, believing everything that is in accordance with the Law and that is written in the Prophets; [15] having a hope in God, which these men cherish themselves, that there shall certainly be a resurrection of both the righteous and the wicked."

And so we see at Revelation 20:12,13 that now all the unbelieving dead of every age of time, starting with Cain at the beginning of creation and of time, are resurrected with a BODY THAT WILL NOW LAST FOREVER to stand before God to answer for one's sins against Him, the foremost being that of unbelief. So when John is led of God to say here at Revelation 20:12, "I saw the dead, the great and the small, standing before the throne," this is a reference to ALL the unbelievers of time, who are now resurrected by God to stand before Him in new resurrected bodies to last forever.

Then when John is led of God to continue at Revelation 20:13, he now digresses to let us know where these unbelievers were coming from, who are all mentioned as one group at Revelation 20:12. And so, when God says, "the sea gave up the dead which were in it, and death and Hades gave up the dead which were in them," God is indicating that the bodies of these dead believers are either coming from "the sea" or from the earth, which is what "death" refers to here. These are the only two places that the physical body of a dead believer could be in time.

Then when God mentions "Hades" giving up the dead that were in them, He is now referring to the soul and spirit of every unbeliever of time being in the compartment of the unbelievers in Hades, which is below the surface of this present earth. The soul and spirit of every unbeliever of time is now seen as coming from Hades to be reunited with one's body coming from either the earth or the sea, to now stand complete before God bodily with soul and spirit, which is the three components of a human being in both time and eternity, as we see at 1 Thessalonians 5:23. And now God gives each of these unbelievers a new body that will not die and will last for all eternity, for now what these unbelievers are all about to experience is eternal death, which is separation from God forever and ever, this being the second death, later mentioned by God at Revelation 20:14.

And when God says at verse 20:12, "the dead were judged from the things which were written in the books, according to their deeds," this is to indicate that God has been keeping track of every single sin ever committed by an unbeliever in time, which were all against Him (noting Psalm 51:4), starting from the time one reached the age of accountability and right up to the time that one died physically.

In contrast to this, God can say to each and every believer of time what we read at Romans 8:1, "Therefore there is now no condemnation for those who are in Christ Jesus." Why? Because each one believed in God's Son during time, namely, that He had died to pay the penalty of death due one's sins and to bear God's wrath due one's sins, when He died at the cross on one's behalf, that is, in one's stead! All of these would therefore have their names written in God's "book of life" mentioned at Revelation 20:12.

However, since this cannot be said of each and every unbeliever of time, who had never come to God for the forgiveness of sins during their stay on earth, then this means that God was keeping track of their sins. The moment one turns to God at salvation, all those sins from the age of accountability onward are instantly forgiven and never remembered by God, or ever brought up again. However, as we see here, this is NOT the case for the unbelievers of time; and now this final judgment of God is the time each one must give God an account of one's life on earth lived in sin, especially for the sin of unbelief!

And what also needs to be remembered in this regard is that unbelievers do receive degrees of eternal punishment in hell, which is why we read about these books, which really contain all deeds done in time, some having been worse sinners than others, due to some living longer to sin more than other unbelievers. This truth here is based on what God says at Revelation 20:12 in the words, "the dead were judged from the things which were written in the books, according to their deeds," and also from what He repeats at Revelation 20:13, "they were judged, every one of them according to their deeds;" and also based on what God says in His word in such passages as Matthew 11:20-24; Luke 20:46,47; and John 19:11. The reality that we must not lose sight of, however, is that every unbeliever of time will still be in torment in hell forever and ever, bar none!

As we continue here, we then see what God does with each of these unbelievers of time, now resurrected bodily, standing before Him in their new resurrected bodies to last forever, to now be given their sentence due their lifelong rejection of God while alive physically on earth, which God now reveals to us in what He says at verses 20:14,15, which we would benefit by noting again here, "[14] Then death and Hades were thrown into the lake of fire. This is the second death, the lake of fire. [15] And if anyone's name was not found written in the book of life, he was thrown into the lake of fire."

What God forever deals with first here is "death and Hades," which are both "thrown into the lake of fire," with this lake of fire being now the fire that we have seen as burning in Sheol/Hades, also known as 'the abyss,' far below this present earth's surface now covering the whole earth, coming up to the surface through the shaft of the abyss (noting Revelation 9:1,2), which is in accord with what God tells us at 2 Peter 3:7, where we read, "But by His word the present heavens and earth are being reserved for fire, kept for the day of judgment and destruction of ungodly men." Since this is now that "day of judgment" then this is now what will occur!

The "destruction of ungodly men" here then refers to what happens next to all the unbelievers of time now resurrected bodily and standing before God, as we see at Revelation 20:15, "if anyone's name was not found written in the book of life, he was thrown into the lake of fire." Other verses of God's word which would be helpful for us to notice here is what God says regarding unbelievers of time and their final destiny at 2 Thessalonians 1:8,9, "[8] dealing out retribution to those who do not know God and to those who do not obey the gospel of our Lord Jesus. [9] These will pay the penalty of eternal destruction (meaning here again loss of wellbeing forever, and not annihilation, that is, out of existence altogether) away from the presence of the Lord and from the glory of His power," and also at Jude 1:7, "just as Sodom and Gomorrah and the cities around them, since they in the same way as these indulged in gross immorality and went after strange flesh, are exhibited as an example in undergoing the punishment of eternal fire." This is a serious outcome indeed!

The word "destruction" that we have seen God use above at 2 Peter 3:7, which is "Apoleia" in the original Greek, refers to loss of wellbeing, not loss of being, such as in annihilation, in reference to being out of existence. Since both angelic beings and human beings are destined to be eternally existing when created by God, then this means that one's final destiny is either in Heaven or hell. God does not teach in His word anywhere the ceasing of existence by either group as time comes to an end and eternity begins!

And as briefly noted at Revelation 20:12, we again have here at Revelation 20:15 God's "book of life," which is the book that God maintains in Heaven, which has written in it the name of every human being in time who has eternal life with Him, due to one believing in His Son for salvation during one's stay on earth, that is, while still alive physically. And as we now see from Revelation 20:15 here, no unbeliever will have one's name written in God's book of life, which means that only one result is possible, which is as we see here, is to be thrown by God into that lake of fire!. What is very important to see here is that THIS IS NOW ETERNAL HELL, where one is in conscious torment, serving the devil forever and ever, away from God's Presence!

That is why God says at Revelation 20:14 here, "this is the second death, the lake of fire," simply because once one is in the lake of fire, such as the devil, his demons, and now every unbeliever of the four ages of time, there is never a coming out of it, which means an eternal separation away from God's Presence, which is NOW A SPIRITUAL DEATH that will last forever and ever!

What also needs to be grasped here is that by every unbeliever of every age of time being raised from the dead, this means that no persons now remains in death, nor in Hades; meaning that no bodies remain in any grave and no souls or human spirits remain in Hades. All the dead of time are raised from the dead, bar none – all believers in stages in the first resurrection, and all unbelievers in what can be called the 'second resurrection,' as we see here – and now what we read at 1 Corinthians 15:26 has its fulfillment, "The last enemy that will be abolished is death." Death will have been abolished for believers with the completion of all stages of the first resurrection, and now here death is abolished completely from God's sight forever with the completion of 'the second resurrection,' when all unbelievers of time are raised from the dead all at once to face God at this final judgment of time!

What is also very important to realize is that no one will ever be able to accuse God of being unfair in the way He deals with unbelievers here, in casting them into the lake of fire, which is eternal hell. For God tells us in His word that it is not His desire to see people perish and be separated from Him forever, for after all, out of love He did send His One and only Son to die for the sins of the whole of the human race.

Let us note again what God tells us for instance at Ezekiel 18:32, "For I have no pleasure in the death of anyone who dies," declares the Lord God. "Therefore, repent and live," and also at 1 Timothy 2:3,4, "[3] This is good and acceptable in the sight of God our Savior, [4] who desires all men to be saved and to come to the knowledge of the truth." In other words, if a human being ends up in hell after the final judgment of God in time, it is because that person made a conscious free choice during one's life on earth to be there; and not because God destined anyone to be there!

So let us never ascribe any blame or unfairness to God in regards to any unbeliever ending up in hell, which by the way only God knows who these are, since God does ensure, during one's life on earth, that one does come in contact with the knowledge of God in some way or other so that NO ONE can ever stand before Him at this final judgment and come up with any excuse! As we see from looking at Revelation 20:11-15 here, God does not mention any unbeliever of time coming up with any excuse, simply because there is none who can ever come up with any excuse!

"For our citizenship is in heaven, from which also we eagerly wait for a Savior, the Lord Jesus Christ; who will transform the body of our humble state into conformity with the body of His glory, by the exertion of the power that He has even to subject all things to Himself."

Philippians 3:20,21

CHAPTER EIGHT

We know that this present earth is not the believer's home due to the mention in God's word of the "city" that God is building for the believers of time, which is not on this earth!

What we now want to do in this chapter is to show that this earth was never meant by God to be the believer's home, due to the fact that throughout God's word believers have been promised a "city" by God, whose builder would be God Himself and which would not to be on this present earth! What this further means is that believers then started looking at themselves as being strangers on this earth, as just passing through, all on one's way to a better country!

That this has been so from antiquity can be seen from what God told the patriarch Abraham, who is believed to have been born almost 4,000 years ago, in 2161 BC, in Mesopotamia, which is present day Iraq, what we now read at Hebrews 11:8-10, "[8] By faith Abraham, when he was called, obeyed by going out to a place which he was to receive for an inheritance; and he went out, not knowing where he was going. [9] By faith HE LIVED AS AN ALIEN in the land of promise, AS IN A FOREIGN LAND, dwelling in tents with Isaac and Jacob, fellow heirs of the same promise; [10] for he was looking for THE CITY which has foundations, WHOSE ARCHITECT AND BUILDER IS GOD."

That this city that God is building for believers during the ages of time is not on this earth is clear from what God goes on to tell believers at Hebrews 12:22-24, where we read, "[22] But you have come to Mount Zion and TO THE CITY OF THE LIVING GOD, THE HEAVENLY JERUSALEM, and to myriads of angels, [23] to the general assembly and church of the firstborn who are enrolled in heaven, and to God, the Judge of all, and to the spirits of the righteous made perfect, [24] and to Jesus, the mediator of a new covenant, and to the sprinkled blood, which speaks better than the blood of Abel."

Since God was speaking to believers of the present third age of time when He spoke what we just read at Hebrews 12 above means that this city that God is building for believers is in Heaven at present, which of course brings up the question of 'when' will God bring believers here on earth to live in that city? And the answer to that question can be found in what God discloses at Revelation 21:10, in the vision that God gave the apostle John while he was on the island of Patmos, around 90 AD, "And he carried me away in the Spirit to a great and high mountain, and showed me THE HOLY CITY, JERUSALEM, COMING DOWN OUT OF HEAVEN FROM GOD." What we are to grasp here then is that the city, as "the heavenly Jerusalem" that God mentioned above at Hebrews 12:22 as being in Heaven, is now seen at Revelation 21:10 as coming down to this earth and being visible from earth, while being just above the earth.

Another detail which is important to bring out here is that Revelation 21:10 – that we read above relating to that holy city, Jerusalem, seen as coming down from Heaven from God – is an event which occurs at the beginning of the fourth age of time, as God's Son, comes to reign over the nations of the earth from that holy city, which is at the second stage of His second coming from Heaven to earth (noting Revelation 19:11-21)!

Then at the end of the fourth age of time, which has a duration of 1,000 years (noting Revelation 20:2,6,7), God's Son hands that kingdom of the holy city, Jerusalem, to His Father (noting 1 Corinthians 15:20-28), which will then become the "new Jerusalem" ON THE NEW EARTH that God then creates for His new creation (being all believers) of time, which is the home of all believers of the four ages of time, and which is now for all eternity to come!

God has this new earth and new Jerusalem in view in what He tells us at Revelation 21:1-4, where we read, "[1] Then I saw a new heaven and A NEW EARTH; for the first heaven and THE FIRST EARTH (of this present original creation) passed away, and there is no longer any sea. [2] And I saw THE HOLY CITY, (now seen as) NEW JERUSALEM, coming down out of heaven from God, made ready as a bride adorned for her husband. [3] And I heard a loud voice from the throne, saying, "Behold, the tabernacle of God is among men, and He will dwell among them, and they shall be His people, and God Himself will be among them, [4] and He will wipe away every tear from their eyes; and there will no longer be any death; there will no longer be any mourning, or crying, or pain; the first things (relating to the original creation) have passed away." That is why the apostle Peter was led of God to state what he does at 2 Peter 3:13, "But according to His promise WE ARE LOOKING FOR NEW HEAVENS AND A NEW EARTH, in which righteousness dwells."

And lastly, before leaving God's mention of the city from Heaven now just above this earth during the fourth age of time, we should make mention of the term "PARADISE," which is ANOTHER TERM FOR "THE HOLY CITY, JERUSALEM, COMING DOWN OUT OF HEAVEN FROM GOD" that we have just had in view at Revelation 21:10, and which God goes on to describe from there to Revelation 22:5! We should also note here that this word "Paradise" occurs only three times in God's word, all of them in the New Testament, which passages we should now look at to show that what has been said above about Paradise is indeed the case.

The first occurrence of the word "Paradise" in God's word is found at Luke 23:43, where we see God's Son, The Lord Jesus Christ, hanging on the cross and about to die, telling one of the thieves also hanging on a cross, who had just believed in Him, what we now read, “And He said to him, "Truly I say to you, today (after you die physically) YOU SHALL BE WITH ME IN PARADISE." Without going into details here (because this concerns death and what happens after death, with the author having written a book to deal with that subject, titled, “Have You Ever Wondered What Happens After Death!”), we are to realize that God’s Son was speaking only of His own human spirit and that of the thief here, and was not speaking of bodily! And so, to keep to our topic, we are to see that where God’s Son was going in spirit was “PARADISE,” which cannot be anywhere else but in the Heavenly city, which, as we will see next, was at that time WITHIN Heaven, as God’s eternal and uncreated abode!

And so, the above becomes clearer still if we now look at the second occurrence of the term “Paradise,” which is at 2 Corinthians 12:4, adding verses 2 and 3 for context, “[2] I know a man in Christ who fourteen years ago — whether in the body I do not know, or out of the body I do not know, God knows — such a man was CAUGHT UP TO THE THIRD HEAVEN. [3] And I know how such a man — whether in the body or apart from the body I do not know, God knows — [4] was CAUGHT UP INTO PARADISE and heard inexpressible words, which a man is not permitted to speak.” And again, without going into too many details here, we are to note that PARADISE HERE IN VIEW IS SEEN AS BEING WITHIN THE THIRD HEAVEN, which is a reference to GOD’S ETERNALLY EXISTING AND UNCREATED HOME!

Then the third and last occurrence of the word “Paradise” is at Revelation 2:7, where we read, “He who has an ear, let him hear what the Spirit says to the churches. To him who overcomes, I will grant to eat of THE TREE OF LIFE WHICH IS IN THE PARADISE OF GOD.” And what we now need to carefully note, in order to see that Paradise is simply another term for that city that God is building for the believers of the four ages of time, is to note what God says at Revelation 22:1,2, where we have God in the process of giving us a description within that city, which He is building, “[1] Then he showed me a river of the water of life, clear as crystal, coming from the throne of God and of the Lamb, [2] in the middle of its street. On either side of the river was THE TREE OF LIFE, bearing twelve kinds of fruit, yielding its fruit every month; and the leaves of the tree were for the healing of the nations."

Since we see from Revelation 22:2 above that the tree of life is clearly seen TO BE IN "the holy city, Jerusalem, coming down out of Heaven from God," that we have in view from Revelation 21:10 to Revelation 22:5; and since we were told that the tree of life was "IN THE PARADISE OF GOD," at Revelation 2:7, then this proves conclusively that "the holy city, Jerusalem, coming down out of Heaven from God" is indeed PARADISE! And this is the city that God is presently building for the believers of time, which will be for all eternity to come on the new earth that God will yet create for His new creation! Readers are encouraged at this point to read God's new creation in time at Addendum C in the back of the book, if one is not familiar with that term!

“The Lord is not slow about His promise, as some count slowness, but is patient toward you, not wishing for any to perish but for all to come to repentance.

2 Peter 3:9

"Do I have any pleasure in the death of the wicked," declares the Lord God, "rather than that he should turn from his ways and live? …For I have no pleasure in the death of anyone who dies," declares the Lord God. "Therefore, repent and live."”

Ezekiel 18:23,32

CHAPTER NINE

A last word!

What is very important to grasp, as we bring this book to a close, is that throughout the ages of time God gives mankind every opportunity to come to believe in His Son and all He has done for us, as human beings here on earth! For starting at Genesis 3:15, right after Adam and Eve had sinned against God, He made known the fact that His Son was coming to earth one day, as born of a woman.

Then throughout the first two ages of time, which goes from Genesis 1:1 to the end of Acts 1, people on earth were saved by believing in God's COMING SON, Who was foreshadowed in the animal sacrifices and offerings! And after God's Son had come to earth and had died at the cross for the sins of all mankind, had been buried, and been raised from the dead the third day, followed by His ascension back to His Father's right Hand in Heaven again, then people are saved by believing in God's Son, WHO HAS NOW ALREADY COME TO EARTH!

And throughout the ages of time, God gave greater and greater revelation of Himself through His word, which He gave to mankind over a period of 1400 years, so that today we have all 66 books of God's word in the Bible. What is also to be observed is that even though not all human beings on earth have a copy of God's written word, God has from the beginning of the original creation never been without a witness on earth of His existence, including the knowledge of how one could come to know Him! What that means is THAT WHEN GOD JUDGES AT THE END OF TIME, NO HUMAN BEING WILL BE ABLE TO STAND BEFORE HIM AND GIVE ANY EXCUSE FOR NOT BELIEVING IN HIS SON WHILE ON EARTH, SO AS TO AVOID THE SENTENCE OF HELL!

For it is important to grasp here is that since the time of God's original creation of mankind on the sixth day of creation, God has given mankind on earth a witness of Himself, for instance through THE EXTERNAL WITNESS OF CREATION, noting here what God tells us at Psalm 19:1-4 in part, where we read, "[1] The heavens are telling of the glory of God; and their expanse is declaring the work of His hands. [2] Day to day pours forth speech, and night to night reveals knowledge. [3] There is no speech, nor are there words; their voice is not heard. [4] Their line has gone out through all the earth, and their utterances to the end of the world...," and also noting what God says at Romans 1:20, where we read, "For since the creation of the world His invisible attributes, His eternal power and divine nature, have been clearly seen, being understood through WHAT HAS BEEN MADE, SO THAT THEY ARE WITHOUT EXCUSE."

And then we are also to observe that God gave all mankind, starting with Adam and Eve, the INNER WITNESS OF CONSCIENCE, so that every human being ever born into this world has written on one's conscience the knowledge of good and evil, which is activated at the time a young child reaches the age of accountability, which is the age known only to God when a young child, who is innocent, not knowing good or evil when born, is tested by God as one now learns for the first time the difference between good and evil, and like Adam of old, now eventually chooses the evil, thereby sinning one's first sin against God and now being under His judgment of death leading to the fire of hell, unless one repents and turns to God to believe in His Son to escape that fire of hell!

Let us note here what God says about that inner witness of conscience that every human being has on earth, even in the darkest continent of earth, first at Romans 1:19, where we read, "...because THAT WHICH IS KNOWN ABOUT GOD IS EVIDENT WITHIN THEM," and also noting what God further says at Romans 2:14,15, where we read, "[14] For when Gentiles who do not have the Law do instinctively the things of the Law, these, not having the Law, are a law to themselves, [15] in that they show the work of THE LAW WRITTEN ON THEIR HEARTS, THEIR CONSCIENCE BEARING WITNESS and their thoughts alternately accusing or else defending them..."

If a human being rejects the first light that God gives all mankind since the beginning, which is His external physical creation that all can see; and if one rejects the inner light of conscience that God gives to every human being born into this world, then it is safe to say that this person will never come to know God.

And the reverse is also true. If a person believes that there is a God due to looking at the physical creation, and if a person still responds to the light of conscience by seeking to adhere to what is right and stay away from what is wrong, based on the dictates of one's conscience, then this is an indicator that the person will at some point before physical death come to personally know God – such as God making His word available so that one can read about His Son, or God sending a believer with the good news of God's Son – all as a work of God's unmerited favor and power alone!

To God alone be all praise, honor, and glory, with thanksgiving, both now and forevermore! Amen, amen, and amen.

ADDENDUM A

/ The four ages of time

What is important to know when reading God's word, the Bible, is that God has divided time into four ages. And since God's word covers all of time, then all of God's word can be subdivided along the lines of these four ages. But before noting what these four ages are, we need to also be aware that in each of the four ages of time, God uses the believers of that age as His vessels. In other words, God is accomplishing His work on earth through the believers of each age of time.

And what is also important to keep in mind in regards to this is that although God starts each age with believers, before long the number of unbelievers in each age outnumbers the number of believers. In other words, one characteristic of each age of time is that there is a believing remnant among a mass of unbelievers, with these believers in each age being those whom God preserves for Himself and through whom God works to accomplish His purposes in each age through time.

And so, in the first age of time God worked through Adam and his believing descendants as His vessels to accomplish His will on earth, which age covers the first eleven chapters of Genesis. What this means is that they were the believers who willingly served Him out of love for Him. In other words, this was the believing line of descent, or the believing remnant, through which God worked out His will.

Then when we begin Genesis 12, we see God take one believer, Abraham, and out of that one man's descendants through the line of Isaac, and then through the line of Jacob, God makes a nation, which is Israel. And again, we need to see that only the believing line of descent within the nation of Israel was the remnant through which God worked to accomplish His will. What this means is that not all those who were of the nation of Israel were believers. In fact, the majority were unbelievers. Therefore, in the second age of time, which goes from Genesis 12 to the end of Malachi in the Old Testament, and includes the gospel accounts of Matthew, Mark, Luke, and John, plus Acts 1 and Revelation 6 to 19 in the New Testament, God works out His will in time through the believers of the nation of Israel, which is again a small number compared to the total number.

And here we need to pause for a moment and mention something else before going on to consider the third age of time, and this is the fact of representation. What this means is that in the first age of time, we have Adam and Eve as our first parents, who were but representative of all people on earth. In other words, God knew that what this one couple did, any other couple would have done the same thing, since God knows that once sin entered His perfect and sinless creation, we all would have the same sinful nature as human beings.

Then the same is true in regards to the nation of Israel in the second age of time, in that God knew that what this one nation did, any other nation on earth would likewise have done had it been chosen by God as a representative nation. So when God set out to make the one nation of Israel, He started out with just believers. But when the nation of Israel came into existence later, only a believing remnant within the nation were believers. Now since the nation of Israel was but representative of all the nations, then God knew that if He had chosen any other nation on earth, He would find that only a believing remnant would ever become believers to serve Him willingly out of love for Him out of a mass of unbelievers, who would now be in any of those nations. In other words, no other human being would have acted any differently than our first parents, and likewise, no other nation would have acted any differently than the nation of Israel did. This means that all human beings and all nations are likewise guilty before God!

What also needs to be mentioned here, as we now go on to look at the third age of time, is that the first two ages basically relate to the time period covered by the Old Testament, which means that the third and fourth ages of time must be covered by the New Testament portion of God's word, the Bible. And let us recall that in the first age, God worked through the believers of that age, beginning with Adam, while in the second age of time, God works through the believers of the nation of Israel, beginning with Abraham. So as we come to the third age of time, which goes from Acts 2 to the end of Revelation 5 in God's word, we have God working through all the believers of earth, whom God calls "the church."

What this means then is that in this third age of time, which we are presently still in, God is accomplishing His will through all the believers of earth, with God now not looking at any specific nation in particular. In other words, during the present third age of time, also known as 'the church age,' the nation of Israel, although being supernaturally preserved by God, is still just the same as any other nation on earth, having a believing remnant among a majority of unbelievers.

Then in the fourth age of time, which is basically covered by Revelation 20 to 22 in the New Testament, although mentioned often in prophecy in various portions of the Old Testament, we have God working through the believers of that age, but now with much greater variation. In other words, during the fourth age of time God works through the believers of every nation on earth still in their natural bodies, and also through the believers of the first three ages of time, who would have now experienced their part in the first resurrection relating to believers and who are now in their resurrected bodies! This is covered in much greater detail in my book, "An Introduction To The New World That Is Coming Upon The Earth," which focuses on this fourth age of time. If there are any readers who are not sure of what is meant by the first and second resurrection, and the fact of people serving God in their new resurrected bodies in the future, please see my book, "Have You Ever Wondered What Happens After Death?"

Before leaving this Addendum, it is also important to be aware that the Old Testament portion of God's word, the Bible, contains 39 books, which deal with the beginning of all things in God's plan of the ages, while the New Testament portion of God's word, the Bible, contains 27 books, which deal with the consummation of all things in God's eternal plan, which God is outworking through the four ages of time.

Also of great value is to know that the second age of time is not completed until AFTER the completion of the present third age of time. In other words, there are seven years remaining in the second age of time dealing with the nation of Israel, which is why this nation is being supernaturally preserved by God during this present third age, simply because God is not yet finished outworking His plan of the ages through the believers of that nation. These seven years remaining is a time of God's judgment against all unbelievers of earth and is approximately covered by Revelation 6:1 to Revelation 19:21 in God's word, although also mentioned often in prophecy in the Bible.

What also needs to be mentioned and is important to remember is that the reason God has a series of ages in time is in order to show us just how sinful the human race is and just how incapable it is of doing good, in terms of pleasing God on its own apart from God. What is meant here is that God's revelation of Himself increases as time progresses, so that those living in the fourth age of time, as compared to the first age of time, will have a far greater knowledge of God.

In other words, as each age progresses, God makes it easier and easier for human beings on earth to come to know Him and to serve Him out of love for Him. For example, in the first two ages, God's precious Son had not yet come to earth, so that He was foreshadowed only through types, such as the animal sacrifices and offerings, and in prophecy. Human beings at that time also only had the Old Testament as light to guide them.

But by the time we reach the fourth age of time, God's precious Son will not only have come from Heaven to earth bodily, but will actually be in the city just above the earth that God will have brought down from Heaven to start the fourth age (noting Revelation 20:10), reigning over the nations as King from there!

Please note what God says at Isaiah 11:9 in part, as just one example of what it will be like in the fourth age, which is something that could not be said in any prior age, "...For the earth will be full of the knowledge of the Lord as the waters cover the sea." What this means then is that when God's final judgment of time comes, relating to all the unbelievers of time (noting Revelations 20:11-15), then none of these unbelievers of time will be able to stand before God and give any excuse for their sin of unbelief, in having personally and freely rejected God's offer of salvation found in His own precious Son, The Lord Jesus Christ. And so, each succeeding age adds to mankind's culpability before a Holy and altogether Righteous God, so that in the end "every mouth may be closed and all the world may become accountable to God" (noting Romans 3:19 in part).

ADDENDUM B

/ The two comings from Heaven to earth of God's precious Son, our Lord Jesus Christ

Another very important truth to know here is that God's word, the Bible, mentions two comings of God's precious Son, The Lord Jesus Christ, from Heaven to earth. His first coming from Heaven to earth was for the purpose of taking on a body like ours, only in the innocence of Adam and as born of a virgin, so as not to incur our sinful nature; and then after living thirty-three and half years on earth carrying out only the will of God His Father in absolute sinlessness out of love for Him, was given over into the hands of unbelievers to be put to death on a cross, before being buried, then resurrected from the dead the third day. And of course, His death was not due to anything God's precious Son, The Lord Jesus Christ, had ever done wrong, but rather was to pay the penalty due the sins of the whole human race, which was death, in order that God might have a basis by which to forgive the sins and grant eternal life to those who come to believe in Him.

Then the second coming of God's precious Son is to be seen as being in two stages. The first stage of His second coming is at the end of this present third age of time, and is for the purpose of bringing to Heaven all believers of earth before God's judgment falls on the unbelievers of the earth, thereby bringing the present third age to a close. God has this first stage in view especially at 1 Thessalonians 4:14-17, although also mentioned in many portions of the New Testament.

Then the second stage of the second coming of God's precious Son, The Lord Jesus Christ, occurs at the end of the seven years of God's judgment, which will end the second age of time. God's precious Son would now be coming for one key battle against God's foes, as led by the devil, before establishing His reign on earth as King during the fourth age of time. This is again disclosed by God in many portions of God's word in the New Testament, but especially in passages such as Matthew 24 and Revelation 19:11-21.

ADDENDUM C

/ God's new creation in time

A very important truth to know here is that God is building a new creation through His Son in time, which consists of all believers of the four ages of time! Just as God brought about His original human creation through the first man, Adam, during the time of the first covenant; now God brings His new human creation into being through His Son, as "the last Adam" and "the second Man" (noting 1 Corinthians 15:45,47), as part of God's new covenant. So just like the first human creation that God brought into being was a physical one; we will now see that this new human creation that God is now bringing into being is a spiritual one!

And now in this Addendum we will look at the fact of there being a new creation of God; then show that God's Son, The Lord Jesus Christ, is the basis for God's new creation; before showing when this new creation of God begins and ends; and then closing by showing God's new heaven and earth as being the eventual home of God's new spiritual creation!

1) The fact of a new creation of God

First then, let us note that just as there was an original physical human creation from God in time, as is clear from what God tells us at Mark 10:6, "But from the beginning of creation, God made them male and female," then there is also a new spiritual human creation from God, noting what

God tells us at 2 Corinthians 5:17, "Therefore if anyone is in Christ, he is a new creature; the old things passed away; behold, new things have come," and also at Galatians 6:15, "For neither is circumcision anything, nor uncircumcision, but a new creation." There had to be an original human creation for there to be a new spiritual creation, and there was, as we have just seen.

2) God's Son, The Lord Jesus Christ, is to be seen as the basis for God's new human spiritual creation!

Then secondly, just as the whole of God's original creation, including humans, came into being through God's firstborn, that being His Son, The Lord Jesus Christ, as we see from Colossians 1:15-17, "[15] He (The Son of God) is the image of the invisible God, the firstborn of all creation (in terms of being first to appear on the scene, that is, in terms of The eternal Son coming forth from eternity into time, by Whom His Father then created all that came into being as part of the original creation, including human beings). [16] For by Him all things were created, both in the heavens and on earth, visible and invisible, whether thrones or dominions or rulers or authorities – all things have been created through Him and for Him. [17] He is before all things (because eternally existing), and in Him all things hold together."

Then we are to see that the new spiritual creation of God also comes into being through His firstborn, that being His precious Son, noting what God goes on to tell us at Colossians 1:18, "He (The Son of God) is also head of the body, the church; and He is the beginning (of God's new human spiritual creation), the firstborn from the dead (speaking here of the very moment of the resurrection from the dead of God's Son, The Lord Jesus Christ), so that He Himself will come to have first place in everything," from that moment on and into all eternity to come!

Another passage of God's word which we need to note here, because it also speaks of God's eternally existing Son being the firstborn of both the original physical creation and also of God's new spiritual creation is Hebrews 1:6, where we read, "And when He (God The Father) AGAIN brings the firstborn into the world, He says, "And let all the angels of God worship Him." What is very important to note is that when God says "again" here, He is saying that His own eternally-existing Son was first seen in the world at the time of the original physical creation, when God The Father created all that exists in the original creation through His Son by The Holy Spirit, as we have seen at Colossians 1:15-17 above. And then He brought His Son into the world a second time, this being at the time when He took on a body as human beings have, but born of a virgin woman in the innocence of Adam, so as not to incur our sinful nature, as we see for instance at John 1:14, "And the Word became flesh, and dwelt among us, and we saw His glory, glory as of the only begotten from the Father, full of grace and truth," and also at Hebrews 10:5, "Therefore, when He (God's Son) comes into the world, He says, "Sacrifice and offering You have not desired, but a body You (God The Father) have prepared (in the womb of the virgin named Mary) for Me" (The Son of God).

3) Seeing when God's new spiritual creation through God's Son actually begins and is completed in time

And then as to the question of WHEN does God's new spiritual creation through His Son actually BEGINS and is COMPLETED in time, we need to look at what God tells us at 1 Corinthians 15:45-49, "[45] So also it is written, "The first man, Adam, became a living soul." The last Adam (speaking here of God's Son, The Lord Jesus Christ, at His first coming from Heaven to earth) became a life-giving spirit. [46] However, the spiritual is not first, but the natural; then the spiritual. [47] The first man is from the earth, earthy; the second man (in reference to God's Son) is from heaven. [48] As is the earthy, so also are those who are earthy; and as is the heavenly, so also are those who are heavenly. [49] Just as we (as believers) have borne the image of the earthy, we will also bear the image of the heavenly."

And so, we see here that God's Son, Who came from Heaven to earth to take on a human body at the time of the Incarnation, that is, at the time of His embodiment in human flesh, which is the moment God The precious Father conceived a body in the womb of Mary, while yet a virgin, is here called "the last Adam" and also "the second man" in relation to God's new human spiritual creation, in contrast to the first man of the original creation, that being Adam! Then we are also told here by God that just as all human beings "have borne the image of the earthy, so will we also (as those who are believers among human beings) bear the image of the heavenly."

And in regards to this "image of the heavenly," which it is clear from the context that God's Son came to earth to bring, we must also note what God says at Romans 8:29, "For those whom He foreknew, He also predestined to become conformed to the image of His Son, so that He would be the firstborn among many brethren," where we learn that all those chosen of God in eternity past for salvation in time, who are here "those whom He foreknew," are "also predestined to become conformed to the image of His Son," which begins at the time of one's justification, when one comes to personally know God in salvation, but will not be completed until the time of one's glorification, which is when one enters God's Presence as now "spiritual," that is, where one now bears "the image of the heavenly" forever, with a body changed to a spiritual body and with the sinful nature removed from the soul.

Then another passage which needs to be noticed here is what we read at John 12:23,24, "[23] And Jesus answered them, saying, "The hour has come for the Son of Man to be glorified. [24] Truly, truly, I say to you, unless a grain of wheat falls into the earth and dies, it remains alone; but if it dies, it bears much fruit." And what The Lord Jesus Christ meant by "the hour has come for The Son of Man to be glorified," is that the time had arrived for Him to enter His Father's Presence in Heaven again at the ascension, in reference to Acts 1:9-11, which event, as we see from verse 12:24 above, could only occur after a physical death and resurrection from the dead. In other words, the physical body that The precious Father gave His Son in the womb of the virgin thirty-three years before would now die at the cross, be buried, and then be raised from the dead the third day. However, when raised from the dead the third day, it would now be as a glorified body, that is, as a body which although visible would nevertheless be spiritual, which will be so forever in His Father's Presence!

And so, the only way that believers, as those who are chosen of God for salvation, can ever be conformed to the image of God's Son, The Lord Jesus Christ, is also through physical death and glorification, that being through a resurrection from the dead, if one has died, or a translation to a spiritual body, if one has not died (noting for instance 1 Thessalonians 4:14-17 here), when one's time of glorification comes. One passage we can note here is Philippians 3:20,21, "[20] For our citizenship (as believers) is in Heaven, from which also we eagerly wait for a Savior, The Lord Jesus Christ; [21] Who will transform the body of our humble state into conformity with the body of His glory, by the exertion of the power that He has even to subject all things to Himself." When that happens, that is, the moment of our glorification, then we as believers will "bear the image of the heavenly," which God's Son, The Lord Jesus Christ, already bears and which He made possible for all believers of time!

Therefore, as to "when" the new creation begins and is completed, we can say that for God's Son, The Lord Jesus Christ, the new creation began at the moment of His Incarnation, but was not completed until the moment of His glorification, which is when He was raised from the dead the third day after His death at the cross and burial. And so, in the same way for those among human beings chosen of God for salvation, which are all those who come to know God in a personal relationship in salvation in every age of time, one becomes part of God's new creation at the moment of one's salvation, which is justification, but which is also not completed until one's glorification, when one's sinful nature is removed and one is given a new spiritual body to live forever in God's Presence!

And so to summarize, as we have been told by God at 1 Corinthians 15:46 above, namely that "the spiritual is not first, but the natural; then the spiritual," so we are to see that just as God's own Son took on our humanity as born of a virgin in the innocence of Adam, whereby God The Father eternally united His eternally existing Son with a human body provided by God, as the last Adam, to begin a new human spiritual creation, and through death, burial, and resurrection from the dead, completed that new creation as the firstborn from the dead, thereby going from the Heavenly to the earthy to the spiritual and Heavenly; then so too with human believers. We, who are the chosen of God, at the moment of one's salvation, which is justification, one who is earthy is united with God through His Son by The Holy Spirit, as the beginning of one becoming a new creation of God, which new creation is then completed at the time of one's glorification, which is when one has the sinful nature removed from the soul and receives a spiritual body for the one of flesh, thereby also going from the earthy to the spiritual and heavenly, so as to live in glory, which is in God's Presence forever!

4) Seeing a new heaven and a new earth as a new creation of God for all eternity of the new human creation of God from time!

What also needs to be observed is that just as God created the original earth, with two heavens (one seen and one unseen, the first created heaven being associated with the original earth, while the second created heaven, which is unseen, is associated with the angels) for His original human creation, then He also will create in the future a new earth for His new human spiritual creation, with its two heavens (one associated with the new earth and the other associated with the unfallen angels), as is clear from what God tells us at 2 Peter 3:13, "But according to His promise we are looking for new heavens and a new earth, in which righteousness dwells," and also at Revelation 21:1-4, "[1\ Then I saw a new heaven and a new earth; for the first heaven and the first earth passed away, and there is no longer any sea. [2] And I saw the holy city, new Jerusalem, coming down out of heaven (which is the third Heaven here, as God's eternal and uncreated abode) from God, made ready as a bride adorned for her husband. [3] And I heard a loud voice from the throne, saying, "Behold, the tabernacle of God is among men, and He will dwell among them, and they shall be His people, and God Himself will be among them, [4] and He will wipe away every tear from their eyes; and there will no longer be any death; there will no longer be any mourning, or crying, or pain; the first things have passed away."

When God says that "the first things have passed away" here, He is speaking of His original creation, which all unbelievers of time are still associated with, but which is here seen to be away from God's Presence eternally! The important information to remember here is that after the fourth age of time, we have the eternal state, which is when God creates a new heaven and new earth, which will be specifically for His new human spiritual creation of time!

“Jesus said to him, “I am the way, and the truth, and the life; no one comes to the Father but through Me.”
“

John 14:6

ADDENDUM D

/ For those who may not as yet know God

Possibly you have been reading this book and have become aware of not knowing this God Who created us and gave us physical life into this world, and up to now has allowed you to live on earth. However, now you do have the desire to know God in a personal way. If this is the case, then this Addendum has been written specifically for you!

And what God wants you to have in coming to know Him is the peace and joy, which comes in knowing that all of your sins committed in your lifetime are forgiven and that you have eternal life with God. And so, your greatest need at the moment is to make peace with God so as to go to Heaven, which is God's home. And so, this Addendum will help to bring that about by pointing you to God so as to come to know Him through faith in His Son, The Lord Jesus Christ.

As we begin, we need to note a most important promise which God makes at Romans 6:23 to all those who do not yet know Him, "For the wages of sin is death, but the free gift of God is eternal life in Christ Jesus our Lord." The good news here is that God offers you eternal life with Him as a free gift, which is to be obtained in His Son, Jesus Christ. What God does not do in this verse from the Bible is tell us 'how' to obtain that eternal life with Him.

Another verse which we can look at where God does let us know 'how' one can obtain that eternal life with Him is noting what God tells us at John 3:16, "For God so loved the world, that He gave His only begotten Son, that whoever believes in Him shall not perish, but have eternal life." Now the added truth which God makes known here is that the eternal life, which He gives to a human being as a free gift, is for those who believe in His Son.

Then the question is: What is it that I am to believe about God's Son, Jesus Christ, which will lead God to give me eternal life with Him forever? And the beauty of God is that He never leaves us guessing, especially when it comes to having a personal relationship with Him, which He desires us to have. Therefore, we should not be surprised when God gives us the answer to our question in what He tells us at 1 Corinthians 15:1-4, "[1] Now I make known to you, brethren, the gospel (which is God's good news regarding His Son) which I preached to you, which also you received, in which also you stand, [2] by which also you are saved, if you hold fast the word which I preached to you, unless you believed in vain. [3] For I delivered to you as of first importance what I also received, that Christ died for our sins according to the Scriptures, [4] and that He was buried, and that He was raised on the third day according to the Scriptures..."

Therefore, "the gospel," which simply means 'good news,' which God wants you to hear and believe in order to "be saved," which simply refers to you coming to know God and have eternal life with Him, is that His Son has already died for you, has already been buried, and has already been raised from the dead again the third day after His death, in order that God would have a basis by which to forgive you of all your sins, which are all against Him, and to freely give you eternal life with Him, for simply believing this message in your heart.

One thing which often prevents a person from believing the gospel at this point is not seeing oneself as a sinner before a Holy God. When we look at ourselves by our own assessment, and especially when we compare ourselves with others around us, we often think of ourselves as being better than others, and so good enough to enter Heaven in our present condition. The problem with this is that it is the product of our own thinking and is not God's assessment of our situation!

God's assessment of our situation is as He tells us at Romans 3:10-12,23 in part, "[10] as it is written, "There is none righteous, not even one… [11] there is none who seeks for God [12] all have turned aside… there is none who does good, there is not even one... [23] for all have sinned and fall short of the glory of God…" Quite a different assessment of the human race from that which we as human beings often have of ourselves, is this not? But why would God have such an assessment of the whole human race? For the answer to that question, we need to be aware that God is Creator of all that exists, so that when God created the first man, Adam, at the beginning of time, God created him in innocence, meaning that Adam as first created by God neither knew good nor evil, nor was there any sin anywhere in God's original sinless creation.

However, the day came when God tested Adam with a command, saying to him in the garden of Eden here on earth, which was the perfect environment which God had for him, what we now read at Genesis 2:16,17, "[16] The Lord God commanded the man, saying, "From any tree of the garden you may eat freely; [17] but from the tree of the knowledge of good and evil you shall not eat, for in the day that you eat from it you will surely die." How important to see here that God gave Adam, who although a real person was also representative of the whole human race, the warning of the penalty of death for disobedience to His command.

Unfortunately, the day did come when Adam did partake of the forbidden tree and thereby did sin against God. The moment that happened, Adam not only became a sinner by practice, but also a sinner by nature. One thing my parents had to continually do while under their care was to restrain me from continually going the wrong way, for it seemed that of myself I could not do good, but kept going into sin. The reason this was happening is that from the age of accountability onwards, I had not only become a sinner by practice, but also a sinner by nature.

And here the age of accountability needs to be seen as being when as a young child in innocence – which moment is known only by God – one comes to learn the right from the wrong and chooses the wrong, thereby becoming personally accountable to God for one's own sin against Him, since all sin is first of all against Him. And that is why God can say at Romans 3:23 above that "all have sinned and fall short of the glory of God," because God knows that all human beings will go the way of Adam, our representative man, which is also why God can say what He does in regards to the whole of the human race at Romans 5:12, where we read, "Therefore, just as through one man (Adam) sin entered into the world, and death through sin, and so death spread to all men, because all sinned" (from the age of accountability onward). And so, we see that the whole human race is declared by God to not only be sinners by practice and by nature from the age of accountability onwards, but the whole of the human race is now subject to death! In other words, in God's sight the whole of the human race is under the judgment of the penalty of death, due to all being sinners by practice and by nature.

You will recall above, in the first verse we quoted from Romans 6:23, God did say there that "the wages of sin is death." And what God means by "death" here is not just loss of physical life, as when the physical body we have dies; but also has spiritual death in mind, which is far worse! Spiritual death has its beginning when a separation takes place between a person and God at the moment one becomes a sinner at the age of accountability and ends after the final judgment of time, when God forever casts away from His Presence those who before physical death refused to believe in His Son, The Lord Jesus Christ, thereby personally forfeiting the forgiveness of their sins and eternal life with God. And now all such will pay the penalty for their own sins in hell, away from the Presence of God forever.

It is in the midst of such a hopeless situation in which the whole of the human race found itself in that God TOOK THE INITIATIVE and sent His own eternally existing Son into the world, as born of a virgin in the innocence of Adam – so as not to inherit the sinful nature passed on from generation after generation from Adam onwards through the conception of the female – so that He might be the acceptable sacrifice offered to God His Father at the cross, there bearing our sins in His body, and there dying the death due our sins! God's Son, Jesus Christ, was then buried and raised from the dead the third day, to ever be alive, for it is through Him, on the basis of what God has done for us through His Son, that God The Father forgives our sins and imparts us eternal life.

Now, by God's grace and His enablement, may you see your need of God's Son to be Your Savior from the penalty due sin, which is death, not only physical, but also spiritual. And by God's grace, may He lead you to believe in His Son, Jesus Christ, and in believing, to receive the forgiveness of your sins and eternal life with God forever! And based on the truth just shared, the author would now like to ask you a few questions, with the answer being just between yourself and God:

When God says at Romans 3:23, "for all have sinned and fall short of the glory of God," does that include you?

When God says at Romans 5:8, "But God demonstrates His own love toward us, in that while we were yet sinners, Christ died for us," were you included in Christ's death on behalf of sinners?

And when God further says at 1 Peter 3:18 in part, "For Christ also died for sins once for all, the just for the unjust, so that He might bring us to God, having been put to death in the flesh, but made alive in the spirit," were you part of the unjust for whom Christ died?

When God says at Romans 6:23, "For the wages of sin is death, but the free gift of God is eternal life in Christ Jesus our Lord," do you want that eternal life as a free gift from God?

When God says at John 3:16, “For God so loved the world, that He gave His only begotten Son, that whoever believes in Him shall not perish, but have eternal life,” do you now believe that Jesus Christ is indeed God’s Son in human flesh, Who came from Heaven to this earth to die in your place, so as to save you from ever experiencing the judgment of God leading to an eternal separation from God in hell?

And when God then further says to you at Isaiah 55:6, “Seek the Lord while He may be found; call upon Him while He is near,” for His further promise to you here is as we read at Romans 10:9-11,13, “[9] that if you confess with your mouth Jesus as Lord, and believe in your heart that God raised Him from the dead, you will be saved (that is, you will now enter into a personal relationship with God by faith); [10] for with the heart a person believes, resulting in righteousness (that is, in now receiving God’s own righteous and eternal life to live by), and with the mouth he confesses, resulting in salvation (that is, in now receiving as a free gift the forgiveness of sins and eternal life with God). [11] For the Scripture says, “Whoever believes in Him will not be disappointed…” [13] for “Whoever will call on the name of the Lord will be saved.” Will you now call upon God from your heart to save you?

The author’s prayer for you at this point, as you now call upon God by His grace, is what we read at Romans 15:13, “Now may the God of hope fill you with all joy and peace in believing, so that you will abound in hope by the power of the Holy Spirit.”

/ The next book

As this book is being published, God has given His servant the go-ahead to write another book, titled “God’s First Letter To The Corinthians.” In case it is not the next book, the reader may want to check with the author’s website to see what book has been published:

http://www.pilgrimpathwaypublications.com

If you have found this book profitable, or any other of the author’s books, please feel free to let family, friends, and co-workers know about this book and the other books. The author is not on any social media sites, so he relies on God and readers to spread the word. May God bless you for doing so!

www.ingramcontent.com/pod-product-compliance
Lightning Source LLC
LaVergne TN
LVHW040946150826
845672LV00002B/561

* 9 7 9 8 8 4 8 8 7 9 9 7 1 *